M000208401

# The 47th Problem Of Euclid In

# Freemasonry

H. P. H. Bromwell

# Kessinger Publishing's Rare Reprints

## Thousands of Scarce and Hard-to-Find Books on These and other Subjects!

- Americana
- Ancient Mysteries
- Animals
- Anthropology
- Architecture
- Arts
- Astrology
- Bibliographies
- Biographies & Memoirs
- Body, Mind & Spirit
- Business & Investing
- Children & Young Adult
- Collectibles
- Comparative Religions
- Crafts & Hobbies
- Earth Sciences
- Education
- Ephemera
- Fiction
- Folklore
- Geography
- Health & Diet
- History
- Hobbies & Leisure
- Humor
- Illustrated Books
- Language & Culture
- Law
- Life Sciences
- Literature
- Medicine & Pharmacy
- Metaphysical
- Music
- Mystery & Crime
- Mythology
- Natural History
- Outdoor & Nature
- Philosophy
- Poetry
- Political Science
- Science
- Psychiatry & Psychology
- Reference
- Religion & Spiritualism
- Rhetoric
- Sacred Books
- Science Fiction
- Science & Technology
- Self-Help
- Social Sciences
- Symbolism
- Theatre & Drama
- Theology
- Travel & Explorations
- War & Military
- Women
- Yoga
- *Plus Much More!*

**We kindly invite you to view our catalog list at:**
**http://www.kessinger.net**

# CHAPTER VIII

## THE 47th PROBLEM OF EUCLID

The Signet of Melchizedek, King of Righteousness and Priest of the Most High God; King of Schalaam, which is King of Peace—the Octalpha or eight fold endless triangle, which, being a geometric figure composed of lines continually reproduced to infinity, by Right Angles, Horizontals, Perpendiculars and Diagonals, was hailed by our Ancient Brethren among all nations, as the Symbol of the Divine Omnipotence, Omniscience and Omnipresence; universal, infinite and eternal.

PLATE X.

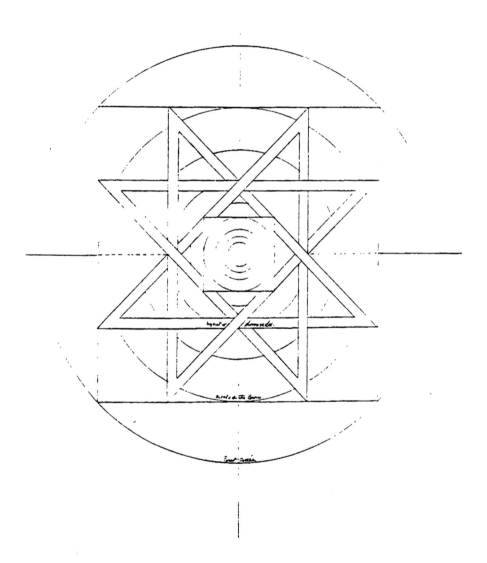

The Octalpha, Master Mason's Floor and Nine Arches (Circles).

# CHAPTER VIII

## THE 47th PROBLEM OF EUCLID

1 ALTHOUGH much has been said in the foregoing chapters concerning the geometric problem known as the 47th of Euclid, and also of its connection with the form and situation of the Lodge, there are reasons for offering some further discussion of the subject in a separate chapter before taking up the floors of the Lodge, which otherwise should be considered as substantially, in some respects, a continuation of the last foregoing chapter.

This course seems to be proper here, not only in order to show more clearly what is meant in parts of the preceding chapters, but to bring out some matters not before mentioned, which will tend, among other things, to manifest the truth of the assertion made in several sections above, that the principles of this celebrated problem constitute the key to Masonic geometry, as it appears in the symbology of the Lodge, not only in respect to external forms, but to the moral and intellectual powers and capacities of man.

2. The particular figure of the problem seen upon the Master's carpet and in the Masonic Monitors shows a right angled triangle, with the longest side (hypothenuse) thereof drawn *horizontally* on the chart or page—the two shorter sides of the triangle, which form the right angle, meeting above; so that these two lines represent the form of the gable of a house with what is called a "square roof." On each of these upper sides is drawn a square, which consequently stands *obliquely* or diagonally to the page, and on the longest horizontal side (hypothenuse), and below, a larger square, which is formed of *horizontal* and *perpendicular* lines, which is the square of the hypothenuse.

This figure in two forms is shown at Nos. 1 and 2 of diagram No. 21, next following.

I mention the perpendicular and diagonal position of the squares of the figure as usually drawn, in order that I may use the terms mentioned, together with the words upper, lower, diagonal, top, bottom, side, etc., to save prolixity of description in making reference to the several parts: Every figure to be used in this chapter being drawn in the same position as that on the Master's carpet, except where more than one such figure are shown together.

3. There are two figures of the problem in common use, one being formed on a triangle, the two shorter sides of which are of *equal* length, as in figure *one* in diagram 21; and the other on a triangle having one of the shorter (upper) sides longer than the other, as in figure two of the same diagram.

The first is the form peculiar to the Master's Lodge—the second, as here drawn, is the form proper to the E∴A∴Lodge, and the same, *reversed* in position, belongs to the F∴C∴, because the form of the Master's Lodge is square and both the others oblong, and also because the squares formed in the one are what Masons call "perfect squares," and those in the others are "oblong squares" throughout.

Although these two forms are all which are possible in triangles having a right angle, and, consequently, are by many supposed to be the only ones which show any particular relation between the squares of the three sides of the triangle; yet there is between the three sides of any triangle, a certain relation by which the *rectangles* or other parallelograms, which may be drawn on them severally, both with right and *oblique* angles (as rhombs), correspond in many respects with the relations between the squares of the sides and hypothenuse of a *right angled* triangle, as will be shown further on.

"4. The matter to be demonstrated in the 47th problem is briefly this (as shown in figures 1 and 2 of said diagram No. 21), that if *any* triangle, as a, b, c, of either of said figures, has one right angle (i. e.: of 90°), as the angle at a in either figure, then, however different the length of the two sides, a, c, and a, b, the squares of those two sides, 1 and 2, added together, will contain precisely the same area as the square of the third side 3. This last mentioned side is called the hypothenuse, and is always the *longest* de, and is so called, because it is usually placed below, as the base line of the *triangle*. If the side a, c, in figure 2 were extended to five or twenty times s existing length, the result would be the same. for the square of the ypothenuse 3, would be enlarged to contain just as much more than the

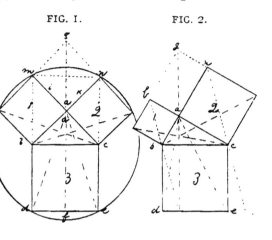

FIG. I.          FIG. 2.

DIAGRAM NO. 21

square 2 of the lengthened side. as would include the square I of the shorter side, which would be then comparatively diminished in a certain proportion to the increase of the square of the longer side.

"Besides, if a right line be drawn from the right angle at *a* perpendicular (at right angles), to the hypothenuse. b, c. it will divide he square of the hypothenuse, 3, into two parts ('oblong squares')—called y geometricians 'rectangles:' and the part on the left side will contain he same area as the square on the left side of the triangle. and the part on ie right side as much as tne square of the right side of the triangle; and iis result always follows, provided the angle be a right angle, whether the ides be equal or not.

"The broken lines in these two figures are those by which the demonstration of the problem is usually made; the *dotted* lines are added for reference urther on. (See Diagram 41, SS., 57-8, of this chapter. *post.*) The *whole* nes are those constituting the figure of the problem."

5. In order to understand the demonstration, several rules in geometry ust first be understood; as that all triangles of equal *base* and equal *altitude* re *equal,* and others. But the demonstration is not needed here, as the object ow is to show those not informed on such subjects, that the large square f the hypothenuse 3, in No. 21, figure I, is equal to the *two* smaller (upper, iagonal) squares marked I and 2, by a simple process, which is as follows: Suppose the lower square 3 (figure I) turned over upwards, so that the

lower corners of it d. e. will come to m and n, at the top (as we are tol
the breast plate of the high priest of Israel was turned up), and it can b
seen that the lower square 3 will cover *one half* of each of the upper diag
onal squares 1 and 2; and also the upper and lower triangles a, m, n, an
a, b, c, which are exactly equal to the *outside* halves of the squares 1 and 2
left *uncovered*, so that the larger square occupies just as much space as th
other two.    This process will not apply to figure 2, where the two sides o
the triangle are *not* of equal length, but only to figure 1.    When this i
carried out in drawing, it will appear as in the next following diagram, No
22, where the square of the hypothenuse is drawn on the *upper* instead o
the *lower* side of the same.    The hypothenuse is the bottom line, marked h
Its square is marked 3, at the center, as in No. 21.

6. In all cases of a triangle, the shorter sides of which are *equal* i
length, this is the simplest form of the figure, for it makes no difference
whether the square of the hypothenuse i
drawn on the upper or lower, the *outside* o
the *inside* of the line.    In this form of th
figure the square is drawn on the *inside* o
the line, and consequently *covers* the righ
*angled triangle* to which it belongs, and
also the triangular space about it, while botl
the other squares are drawn on the *outside*
of their respective lines, but are half covered
by the square of the hypothenuse.    In this diagram, No. 22, 1 and 2 are the
squares of the shorter sides and 3 is the square of the hypothenuse of the
triangle, a, b, c.

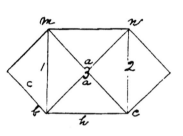

DIAGRAM NO. 22

This form of drawing the figure of the problem is not only simpler than
the usual form, but actually serves as a demonstration thereof, and will
demonstrate it to those who can not understand the other mode; but, as said
above, will not serve in case of a triangle whose shorter sides are unequal in
length, as in figure 2 of diagram 21.

7. In this last diagram, No. 22, the outer halves of the squares, 1 and 2,
would exactly fill the two spaces in the large square not occupied by their
two inner halves; and the *four halves* of the squares 1 and 2 are exactly the

same in size and form as the *four quarters* of the square 3. It can be easily seen that the two diagonal squares 1 and 2 are each the size of a diagonal square which might be *inscribed in* the larger square 3. touching with its four corners the middle of each of the four side lines of the same.   It is also plain to be seen that there are two complete figures of the 47th problem in the last diagram. No. 22. as it is exactly the same when turned *upside down*. and either the top or bottom line is the hypothenuse of a right angled triangle of the same form and dimensions.

8. The next diagram, No. 23. shows the same form of the figure of the 47th problem. drawn *four fold* instead of double. and is formed by only adding to the diagram last shown. No. 22. one half of a diagonal square, that is. a right angled triangle. above and below.   In this figure each of the four lines which form the square b. c, d. e. is also the line of the hypothenuse of one of the four right angled triangles which meet at the *center*—hence the same square is the square of the hypothenuse of each of the last mentioned four triangles which surround it.

Take the lower horizontal line, No. 1. and it is seen to be the hypothenuse of the triangle a, b, c. and its square

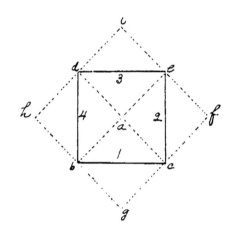

DIAGRAM NO. 23

is formed by the lines 2. 3 and 4. and the squares of the two "sides" of the triangle are d. h, b, a, and e, f, c. a, in the same position as the corresponding squares in the last above figure, No. 22.   Each one of the lines 1, 2, 3 and 4 will be in the same relative position as to every other part. as the figure is turned round.   The four diagonal or oblique squares contain collectively *twice* the area of the large perpendicular square, and form a larger diagonal square, h, i, f, g, as shown by the dotted lines; and the perpendicular square, b, c, d, e, is, as to the dotted square, an "inscribed" diagonal square of *half* its size.

This last figure shows somewhat (but little) of the order of a number of figures of the 47th problem drawn around a center, with the right angles of the triangles meeting at that point—a matter which will be mentioned further on. It also shows how the Master's Apron actually contains a right angled triangle. with the hypothenuse at the *top,* and the square of that hypothenuse.

9. Although there are many books which show the demonstration of the 47th problem. there are none that I know of which *explain* it. or show in any short way how it is that these squares have the relation toward each other that is taught and demonstrated. In order that those who are unskilled in such matters may see the principle of this, I will say here that (as to the figure 1 of diagram 21) it is nothing more than the relation as to length.

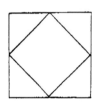

DIAGRAM NO. 24

breadth and area of any square and another which is just large enough to be diagonally (quatre cornered) upon it. and touch with each of its four corners the middle point of each of the four sides of the first. as shown in diagram No. 24.

This is a very simple figure of eight lines, yet it holds the solution of this celebrated problem—so far at least as the figure on the Master's carpet is concerned—and consequently. in a more involved condition. the principle of its various forms.

10. The diagonal square in this diagram. No. 24. is the same as either of the diagonal or oblique squares drawn on the two equal sides of the right angled triangle in figure 1 of diagram No. 21, in this chapter. The larger perpendicular square in this diagram 24 is the same as the square of the hypothenuse in the other; and all the squares of the sides of the triangle in that or any other similar figure of the 47th problem. in which the triangle has two equal sides. are formed by diagonal lines drawn to cut the square of the hypothenuse from corner to corner. This is shown in the next following diagram. No. 25, in which the diagonal square (dotted lines) in the center is manifestly of the same size as each of the other diagonal squares in the figure, *for it laps on four* of them to their *centers,* and so it covers *one fourth* of each, and has the same form and extent in every direction.

11. Now this central diagonal square in the last mentioned diagram No. 25 has just half the area of the square in which it is inscribed. which is the

quare of the hypothenuse in the figure of the problem, a, b, c.  For if the our corners of the perpendicular square not covered by the dotted diagonal quare were supposed to be turned in, they would meet at the center, and xactly cover the diagonal square.   Each perpendicular or right square in he entire diagram is seen to be divided into four quarters by the diagonal ines which cross at its center, and each of these *quarters* is itself the *one half* of a diagonal square. the four being nothing more nor less than the halves of the four diagonal squares which lap over on and meet at the center of he same right square.

But all this is still more plainly seen on *counting* the squares and half squares of both kinds, each set of which actually fills the whole octagonal figure.   There are *five* perpendicular squares and four *halves*, making *seven in all*, and there are *twelve* diagonal squares and four *halves*, making *fourteen* in all: so that no doubt can be felt that the diagonal squares are just *half* the size of the others.

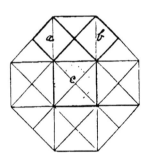

DIAGRAM NO. 25

As to those cases in which the two sides of the right angled triangle are of unequal length, doubtless the same principle governs, but it is not so easily detected.    It is in those forms of the problem that the demonstration lines (broken) seen in figures 1 and 2, in diagram 21, in this chapter. section 3. become necessary.   But let the demonstration be made as it may, in every case in which there is a right angle in the triangle (and there can be but one). whether the two sides form what is called by Masons "the right angle of a perfect square," or of an "oblong square," the squares formed on those sides, taken together, are exactly equal in area to the square of the hypothenuse.

12. Concerning these "oblong" and "perfect" squares, I wish to say here that there are some matters connected with them which every E∴A∴and F∴C∴ought to know, so far as to *his part* in them—and much more every M∴Mason, and particularly the officers concerned in the *first* and *last* sections of *every* Degree.   For many years past the E∴A∴has been the only Mason

taught where his "oblong squares" are to be found, and he is only taught *in part*. Of the *three* foundation stones, and their proper places, the Lodge only know *one*, and there are probably not ten Masons alive in the United States who know, from any *work* they have ever *seen* in a *Lodge*, where or how they stand.

There are two "oblong" and one "perfect square," and each is necessary in *three* places. Two of them are *square* with the *lines* of the Lodge, and one is not and can not be. The per-fect belongs to *two* in the work, and the *squares* of its *hypothenuse* con-form to the lines of the Lodge, that is, to the astronomic lines, and form those of the "Stone of Foundation." He who knows the matters involved in these, knows when, where and how he is on the *center*, the chief lesson in the whole work, with *one* exception. See Diagram No. 5.

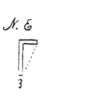

The next following diagram, No. 26, can not be explained here, for rea-sons already mentioned, but the forms and situations shown are of the high-est importance to every Master who would "make ye work perfect." The significations are within the reach of every M∴M∴possessed of "skill and

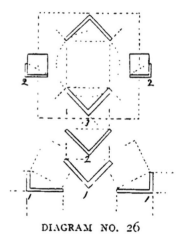

DIAGRAM NO. 26

assiduity," by means of what is shown in other parts of this book, and, moreover, they will be found demonstrable from the "*work*."

13. In the chapters concerning "the Three Great Lights" and "Geom-etry" both the equilateral and right angled triangles are spoken of, and the difference between their respective significations in Masonic symbology partly shown; and also why it is that the right angled triangle is one of the three

Great Lights, and that it signifies the Divine order in creation, as the equilateral triangle is the representative of the "All Producing Cause." In this chapter the right angled triangle only is considered, and this subject involves the square itself, with all its relations to other forms.

The 47th problem of Euclid itself derives its chief importance from the combination and co-ordination of the several squares which are the principal parts of its figure, and elementary parts in the problem, as the same is generally understood, and essential to its exploration. They are necessarily, in position, oblique to each other, more or less, according to the proportionate length of the lines of the triangle on which they are constructed, and which they circumscribe or surround by coterminous lines, or, rather, lines which are each common to the triangle and one of the squares. The triangle is that which *unites* the squares and, as it were, forms them into one complete figure.

14. But, after all, the squares are not in the figure of the problem, nor in the problem itself, except for the purposes of investigation and demonstration—they hold a similar relation to the triangle on whose sides they are projected: that the lines by which the problem is usually demonstrated hold to the squares themselves (for these lines see diagram 21 in this chapter, ante). For the real matter which is to be demonstrated is in the triangle itself; that is, in its lines, for this is is really to be shown, viz., that the relations of the several *sides* of the *triangle* to *each other* are such that, let one of the two sides which form the right angle be lengthened or shortened to any length compared with the other, the third side or hypothenuse will then so lengthen or shorten, as to each of them at the same time, that its *own* square will be as to *both* the others *together*, the *same* as before.

15. The next following diagrams, Nos. 27-28, show this, and the proportionate increase and decrease in the area of the several squares in two classes of cases.

The first diagram, No. 27, is one in which the two *"sides"* are *varied* in length, while the hypothenuse remains the *same*. In this case the square of the side made longer *gains* just as much as the square of the shortened side *loses*, while the square of the *hypothenuse* is, of course, the *same*, for it can

13

not be otherwise, for it is the square of that which remains unchanged. In this figure the squares a. a, and a, a, go together; so with b. b, d. d, and the rest.

16. The next diagram, No. 28, shows the left hand side of the triangle shortened as the right side is lengthened, but not in the same manner as in the last figure. Here the *right angle* of the triangle keeps its position through all the changes, while the *hypothenuse* becomes *longer* at every change. Instead of the squares on the right side gaining just as much in surface as those on the left side lose, it will be seen by the small dotted squares on each side that in the first change, while the left square, a, loses *seven* dotted squares, the right hand square, a, gains *nine;* and on the next change the left side, b, loses *five,* and the right. b, gains eleven; and on the next and last change the left. c, loses *three* and the right c, gains *thirteen;* so that on the whole the area of the two squares of the sides of the triangle is greatly increased. while the squares of the hypothenuse are also increased in exactly the proper proportion to both the

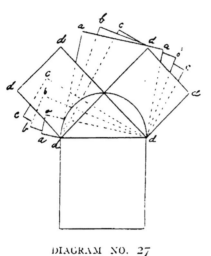

DIAGRAM NO. 27

others. It will be seen that the changes in this case cause a revolution of the entire figure around the center of the square of the hypothenuse, and that all the squares of the hypothenuse keep the same center.

The squares marked a, a, a, go together to form one figure of the 47th problem; so, also, with b, b, b, and the rest. (See diagrams Nos. 27 and 28.)

17. From these, and other similar figures which may easily be constructed. it may be seen in some measure that, whatever there may be of value in the principles of the 47th problem, they are inherent in the *triangle,* and that the squares, as well as lines which make up the whole figure, are really but means of demonstration of their existence; that is, when used to form this particular figure. But, aside from this, the square has properties equally remarkable—and this is not to be deemed inconsistent with what is said

above; for every *"square" consists* of *two* or more right angled *triangles;* that is, as many as one may choose to make by subdivision.  The first division by a diagonal line forms *two*—hence every "perfect square" may be said to consist of *two* right angled triangles of *equal sides;* and every "oblong square" of two right angled triangles of unequal sides, and of these are formed all the squares and right angled parallelograms ("oblong squares") in the universe.  Indeed, all other figures whatever are formed of these— that is, of these or other triangles, and every one of the latter, whatever its form, may be divided into *two right angled triangles.*  But, as is said in the chapter concerning the three "Great Lights," there is but *one* equilateral triangle, wherefore it has the most sublime signification of all figures possible in symbolic or Masonic geometry.  As there may be many right angled triangles, their difference is altogether in the difference in length of the lines which form the sides, not in the right angle.

18. The next following diagram, No. 29, shows the 47th problem, with a right angled triangle of equal sides, together with the circle which circum-

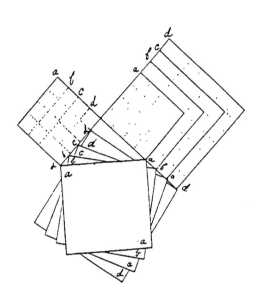

DIAGRAM NO. 28

scribes it, cutting all the external angles of the figure; and the next thereafter following, No. 30, shows why it is that this circle touches all the angles, and why it has its center on the middle of the hypothenuse line.  The use of this circle is, among other things, to *"prove* the *work"* (not to *demonstrate* the *problem*), that is, to prove that the figure is perfectly formed.

In *Masonry* this circle *belongs* to the figure, not only because the proportions of the border of every floor arise from this, but because the circle is the most comprehensive figure possible in geometry, and the one in which all other figures, including the triangle, are contained; and this gives it a high signification in Masonic symbology, especially in connection with the triangle, of which all other forms (including the circle) are composed: and in consequence of this, the compasses are also of high significance, as shown in the chapter concerning the "Three Great Lights."

For these and other reasons the circumscribing circle, although it may well be dispensed with in geometric operations (except in drawing the figure, yet in Masonry, when the 47th problem is set forth for *symbolic* purpose it should not be displayed without so significant a member of its figure as its *enclosing* circle, and *test* of its proper form.

19. Any skillful Mason, whose attention may be called to the matter, can see on a moment's inspection of this diagram, No. 29, that it is a perfect picture or representation of *Masonry* itself in its three Degrees.

Of the two upper squares drawn on the side lines which form the right angle of the triangle a. one square, marked 1, represents the *first*, and the other, marked 2, represents the *second* Degree of Masonry. These are in many respects substantially equal or parallel Degrees, as the two Degrees of man, the will and understand-

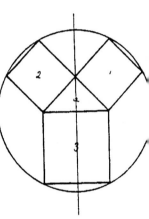

ing—and the *centers* of these squares are on the two *tropical* lines which are the side lines of the square of the hypothenuse. The square 1 and 2 are formed on the two sides of the right angled triangle while on the third (hypothenuse) side thereof is formed the third or *Master's* square (3). The first and second differ from the third square particularly in this, that they are *necessarily* formed *obliquely* to the center line, to wit, the *equator*, so-called because it is the line of *equality*, of *equilib rium*, the *median* line of the *earth*, and of the *Lodge* of which the earth is the *"ground floor."* Their form and *situation*, as to the equator and meridian is the same as of the stones of the *mosaic work* of the *pavements* of the *first* and *second* Lodge floors. On the opposite side of the triangle, which side is *square* with the *equator* and *parallel* with the "high meridian," is the *"Master's* square," which is *necessarily* square with both the *equator* and the *meridian,* and in *position* corresponds thereto in the very same manner as the stones of the *Master's* floor.

This square is equal in area to *both* the *oblique* squares, and is *"on the center."* It is the floor of the *Master's Lodge.* It is the consummation and *completion* of the *whole.* There is no space or place for any *other* square, nor for any other *Degree,* for the *circle circumscribes all* exactly, and is as a *bond* and seal of *unity* and *universality* (both of which are its significations) on the *complete work,* and *proves* the work, that it is *true* in *all* its parts. Moreover, it is the square of the R∴Arch Breastplate.   (See diagram 38, section 45, of this chapter.)

20. The *middle* of the hypothenuse is the *center* point of this *circle* and of the problem in its more ample form, as will appear further on.  To many persons this appears to be out of order, because they think the center should fall on the center of the *triangle;* and that, therefore, there is lacking something of the apparent perfection of order which this remarkable figure otherwise presents.

But this view of the matter is dissipated at once on examining the next diagram, No. 30, which is the same figure in a more *complete* form; that is, it shows the figure *complete* and of the same size as in No. 29, in *four* different projections, with *eight* other complete figures of the same problem, but of *half* the size, *all within* the *same circle* which incloses the *one* figure in No. 29.

21.  In looking at this diagram, No. 30, one sees the figure of the problem drawn with the square of the hypothenuse at the bottom; turn it upside down and the complete figure appears in corresponding lines, and the same appears on looking at it from either side; so that there are four complete figures of the larger size.   Then, taking it diagonally, *two* such figures in the *same* position appear, one above the other, and it is the same as seen from each of the four corners, e h, g f, a d and b c, making in all *eight* complete figures of the 47th problem of *half* the size of those first mentioned, *twelve* in all.

Of these, four are placed each with the *right angle* of its triangle at the center, and the square of its hypothenuse at one of the corners mentioned, and the other four have each the center of its square of the hypothenuse at the center of the whole figure.   In this form of the octagon the squares of its *longer sides,* a. b. and the others contain each just twice the area of the square of any one of the *shorter* sides, as b c. h e. and the others. The letters in this figure show the places of the *twelve jewels* in the *breastplate* of Aaron. (See sections 45 to 51. diagrams No. 38-9-40. showing how these stones are on the *centers* of the *stones* of the *Master Mason's floor;* also large plate IV.)

22. Now the point in the middle of the hypothenuse line in the last preceding diagram. No. 29. appears here in the *center* of *everything.* The *triangle* in the former diagram, 29. appears here as *half of a square,* i. j. k. l. divided diagonally to form *two* triangles. and divided again at right angles to form the same division.    Hence.
the same square contains, in fact, *four* of the larger triangles, with the middle of each hypothenuse line on the *center* of the *circle;* and four of the smaller triangles, with the *right angle* of each at the same center.    And the central square. which is diagonal. is the center of the larger perpendicular square which incloses it. and also the center of the entire complex figure, which fills the circle.

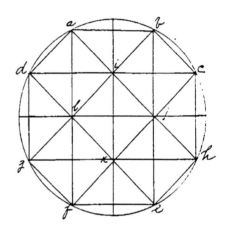

DIAGRAM NO. 30

23. Although the last diagram is of the same size as the one last preceding it, and has but few more lines. it contains *five* large squares of the same size as the square of the hypothenuse in that single figure—*five* squares *half* as large—*twelve* squares *half* as large as these last—*four* large right angled triangles—*sixteen* of half the size of these—*twenty-four* others of *half* the size of the last; and *twenty-eight* others of half the size of these—all forming *twelve* complete figures of the 47th problem of Euclid as seen on the Master's carpet—the same number as that of the stones of the breastplate. and of the *even* numbered stones of the Master's floor on which they are placed.    (See diagrams 38 and 39. sections 45 to 52. post.)

And this is the result of tracing *one* complete figure about the center of the circle. without doing more than to extend its few lines across the circle.

and add two long and three short lines, which serve for its *demonstration* in lieu of those usually drawn, and without introducing any lines not necessary for that purpose.   (Plates X and XI.)

24. But there is another matter in this diagram, No. 30, which may be overlooked.   It contains (as No. 25) that remarkable figure which may be properly called the Octalpha—the endless *eight* pointed triangle, which. being itself a *four fold* figure of the 47th problem (which can be made to appear on examination), and whose lines, like those of the pentalpha and heptalpha and other endless triangles, continually return upon themselves, has, in geometric symbology, the same signification of *infinity* and of *eternity*.

The lines in this diagram, No. 30. which form the octalpha. are traceable, beginning at any of the eight outside angles, as at *a*. thence to h. g, b, e, d, c. f. a. and so on.

Besides this. the lines mentioned are doubtless those which give the order of position of the *twelve jewels* in the *Breastplate* of *Aaron*, which order, like that of the octalpha and 47th problem. is a combination and disposition of the *odd* and *even* numbers to the number of *completion*, which is *twelve*. These odd and even numbers are the ternary and quaternary—the triplex and quadruplex—in geometry the *triangle* and *square—quadrangle*.   They are *added* together in *seven*, the number of *perfection;* and *multiplied* together in *twelve*, the number of *completeness*—completion relating to the *process*, and completeness to the *subject*.

25. The order of position of the twelve jewels is well known—"*four rows*, and *three* in a row;" that is, two rows *perpendicular* and two *horizontal*. The places of the jewels according to this order are shown in diagram No. 30, at a, l, f—b, j, e—d, i, c—g, k, h—in the cornerings of the diagonal (second-ary) squares and small perpendicular squares, and in the centers of the large or prime perpendicular squares, and at the eight angles which are the points of the octalpha.   But this will be further shown in sections 45 to 52 of this chapter, concerning the breastplate, at large.

26. The matters above spoken of are somewhat further shown in the next following diagram, No. 31. which contains the octalpha and some different combinations of the figure of the 47th problem, and also some illustrations of the formation of such figures around a center.   But it is very incomplete

in respect to the latter, as the smallness of the figure permits but a few line
to be shown without causing confusion.   But it contains not less than fort;
eight complete figures of the 47th problem. the greater part of which a:
different in position from any of those contained in the foregoing figure
though the principal lines are the *same*, save that the *spaces* between the:
are made *equal,* so that the eight sides of the octagon are of *equal lengt/*
This produces changes through-
out the figure.   All the angles
formed are of 45. or one of its
multiples. 90 or 135. degrees.

27. In these figures the
"Greek Cross" and "Saltire
Cross" or "Cross of St. Andrew"
appear in several forms. ( Plates
XII. XIII. XIV and XV.) These
are not only symbols in Masonry.
with more significance that has
been yet explained. as far as I
know, but they are the mathematical signs of *addition* and
*multiplication,* and the latter is

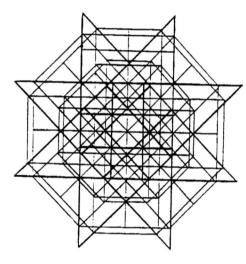

DIAGRAM NO. 31

the sign of *"blessing* and *abundance."* and is the same given by Jacob i:
blessing the sons of Joseph : and the former contains all right angles, horizon
tals and perpendiculars.

28. As it has been shown in part that the principles of the 47th problen
reside primarily in the *triangle* itself. around which are grouped the square:
for the purpose of making the same manifest, we might go further and shov
that all there is in the triangle for the purposes of this problem is inheren
in the *right angle;* and it may be seen that this is not far from the truth or
reflecting that it makes *no difference* to the result how greatly the lengths
of the *lines* may be varied, as long as the *right angle* is maintained.   The
*lines* may vary in *length,* but, while the *right angle* remains, the *proportion*
which the *two* squares of its sides maintain in relation to the *third,* or square
of the hypothenuse. *remains constant.*

PLATE XI.

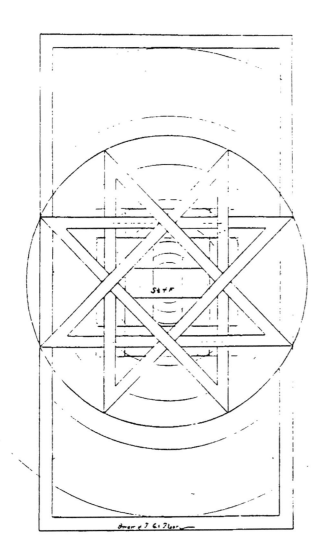

The Octalpha, Master Mason and Fellow Craft Floors,
With Eight Arches (Circles of Enoch).

29. This may serve in some measure to show why it is that the *angles* in any figure (that is, the degrees therein contained) fix the geometric value or character of such figure, and consequently its *symbolic* value in *Masonry*.

It is plain now to any one who reflects that the angles involved in the figure of the 47th problem, with triangle of equal sides, when drawn in its ordinary form or in the more simple form shown above, or in any of the more complicated forms lastly shown, whether the most acute or most obtuse which may arise from their various combinations, are in proportion or ratio to each other as a series of 2, 4, 8, 12, 16, 24, and so on, corresponding with a division of the circle into parts of 90, 60 or 45 degrees, or their divisions by an even number.

This is the same proportion as that between the extensions of the Lodge floors, as to length and breadth, and will doubtless be true in drawing any number of squares, as 4, 8, 16, 32, or other number divisible by four, equally distributed around a center. The dimensions of the *stones* in the several *foundations* of each floor, and in the several courses or layers of the *floors* of all the Lodges, are in the same proportion to each other as the *squares* and *subdivisions* thereof in the figure of the 47th problem; nor would it be possible to lay the foundations or floors with stones of any other proportions, as may be seen in the chapter on "The Floors of the Lodge," sections 10 and 23 to 26.

30. As the floor of the Master's Lodge is formed by the square of the hypothenuse of *one* right angled triangle in the figure of the 47th problem, so the floor of the F∴C∴Lodge is formed by *two* such squares in *two* figures of said problem, whether drawn in the ordinary form or in the more simple form shown in diagram No. 22, as will appear on examining the next following diagram, No. 32, which is the same as No. 22 doubled. In this latter figure the square of the hypothenuse is drawn on the side of the same opposite that usually chosen, but, there being two figures whose squares of the hypothenuse occupy the *same place*, it makes no difference, as can be seen on inspection. For if this diagram were cut in two on the perpendicular line a, a, each half would be a complete figure of the 47th problem, the same as No. 22, and double also (for there are *four* in the entire figure), as there are *two* in No. 22. But, taking it as a whole, it consists of *two figures* drawn in *the*

*usual* form. The large square on the left, with the figure 2 on its center, the square of one hypothenuse; and the two diagonal squares on the right marked 2, 2, are squares of the two sides of the triangle c; and the three together, with the triangle c, constitute one figure. The large square on the right, marked 3, and the two diagonal squares on the left, marked 3, 3, and the triangle d, constitute the other figure. But this floor as fixing the form of the Lodge as to *height* will be examined further in the chapter concerning the F∴C∴Lodge, sections 7 to 14.

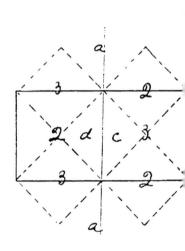

DIAGRAM NO. 32

31. It will be seen that the dotted lines in this figure form a regular saltire cross, or cross of St. Andrew, which is of the same proportions as the third or inmost one shown in diagram No. 31. also Plate No. XVI, which contains four or more forms each of the saltire and Greek crosses. This inner cross in that figure, with bars three times as long as wide, which contains one set of the squares of the hypothenuse of the smallest triangle there shown; the square in each end of the bar occupying one third its length, and the two small triangles in the center the other, or middle third.

It is the same with the Greek cross there shown. It may also be seen that the square of the hypothenuse in the small central figures, with the right angled triangle on which it is drawn, which touches the *center*, gives the precise form of the front elevation of the Tabernacle of Moses, and indubitably of the completed Holy of Holies, standing within the solid stone enclosure of the "House," in the Temple of Solomon; and also the true form of the Master Mason's apron, long cast aside, but now being generally restored; also the figure of the Masonic banner, suspended by its cords, and particularly the W∴Master's *jewel* and apron, as worn in all Lodges.

32. It is this form which gives their relative proportions to the squares, oblongs, circles, triangles, octagons, hexagons, and the rest, which make up the combinations in the extended and multiform diagrams which may be

drawn to illustrate the principles involved in the 47th problem. And it can be seen from such illustrations that the figure formed by the combination of the second and third Great Lights, when disposed according to their proper and *two fold* order—to wit, the combination of the *equilateral* and *right angled* triangles, contains the principle, and, as it were, the *germ* of all these forms. And, further, that the combination of the equilateral and right angled triangles, in respect to their order and its results, correspond throughout with the combinations and complications of the two numbers *three* and *four*, in the science of numbers. That is, the numbers *two* and *three*, for four is only the *square* of two, that is, *two* times *two* or two *twice* expressed, and the *square* of any number has for this reason the *same* symbolic signification as the number itself, but intensified or emphasized by this reiteration of the idea. And the several series of odd and even numbers flow in order from these two, as the countless varieties of *forms* flow from the equilateral and right angled *triangle*.

33. If this can be seen in the forms of the combinations produced by the positions to the second and third great lights, it is still more clearly discovered in the forms and combinations of the *three*, when taken in connection with *three* certain *squares* with which all M∴Masons are familiar, but which are never thought of in connection with them, or with anything else, but only as mere *appropriate* figures to fill up what would otherwise be a gap in a ceremony. Concerning this subject, it is not advisable to say more in this place than that they are connected with the floor work, which, in the second and third instance, is left *incomplete,* as only *one* foundation stone is thought of, and the situations and positions of the other two overlooked.

34. As the three *squares* of the *work* are each connected with its proper form of the figure of the 47th problem, and as these three in their *first, second* and *last* position, are co-ordinated to teach three of the great *lessons* of the Lodge, they have been shown in their proper disposition in diagram No. 26 in this chapter, and now they shall be further shown in different forms, according to order. If any one is in search of something that has been lost (not the G∴O∴W∴), he can find several matters in the diagram last referred to, and in the three next following, which will be worth his *attention* and

an effort to restore. I restored the matters indicated in the diagrams referred to, twenty-nine years ago, and maintained them six years, while Master of two Lodges. They are shown by the geometric order to be proper, and more than that, they are actually *wanting* to *finish* what is already begun in *all* Lodges, and which is carried on *in part,* to this day, and it can be seen, from old allusions and drawings, that they were formerly well understood and put in practice, and the same is the case with the matters shown in this last diagram. (See diagrams Nos. 5, 26 and 33.)

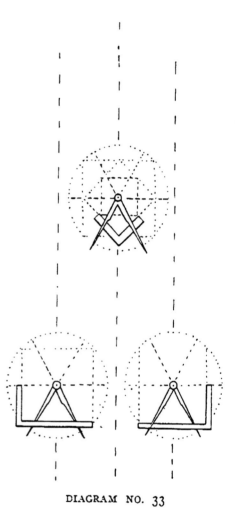

35. All that has been so far mentioned in this chapter is connected more or less directly with the right angle of *equal* sides or limbs, but the principles of the problem in question extend to all triangles which have one *right angle,* whether or not the two "sides" be of the same length.

Thus, the familiar rule of carpenters and masons, known as the rule of *six, eight* and *ten,* is only an application of this principle to a right angle having one side or limb longer than the other, in the proportion of *six* to *eight,* or, what is the

DIAGRAM NO. 33

same, *three* to *four* or *twelve* to *sixteen,* and so on. The reason why *six* and *eight* are chosen for this purpose is that when the two sides of the angle are severally in length six and eight, or other whole numbers in the same proportion to each other, the diagonal (hypothenuse) is always a *whole number,* so there are no fractions.

36. Now, if any one will *square* these three numbers he will see that the 47th problem is true in one class of cases at least, for six times six make *thirty-six*, and eight times eight make sixty-four—these are the squares of the two sides which form the right angle, as at the corner of a house; and these two square numbers, thirty-six and sixty-four, make an even *hundred;* and the diagonal line or hypothenuse is *ten,* the square of which is *one hundred.*

The innumerable ways in which this principle is brought into use in geometric and other mathematical processes for the solution of difficult problems may be found in books devoted to those subjects—they need not be here further considered.

37. But, besides the right angled triangle of *equal* or of *unequal* sides, which have been mentioned, there are two other cases—those are an acute or obtuse angle, with two *equal* sides or limbs, and such an angle with its two side *un*equal.

Concerning the first of these last mentioned cases, it was said above in this chapter that, although *squares* formed on the two shorter sides would not together be equal to the *square* of the longer side, which answers to the hypothenuse in right angled triangles, yet *parallelograms* may be formed with angles corresponding to the angle formed by the two sides, which together would be equal to a parallelogram of right angles ( rectangle) whose direct (perpendicular) length should be equal to the diagonal (perpendicular) extent of the two first, as in figure 1, diagram 34, next following.

38. In the first class of cases above mentioned—those of a *right angle* of equal sides, the parallelograms being not only *rectangles,* but *squares,* the *diagonal* length of the lesser squares was in every instance exactly equal to the *length* and the *breadth* of the larger square, because such diagonal length was always the same as that of the hypothenuse. So in this case (supposing that the large rectangle D is drawn perpendicular), although the *perpendicular* extent of the two diagonal parallelograms, e and f, may not be the same as the length of the hypothenuse, the *horizontal* diagonal of each smaller parallelogram will be; and the perpendicular length of each will be the same as the perpendicular of the larger parallelogram or rectangle; and the two smaller parallelograms will be equal to each other: and both together will

be equal to the third or larger, as the corresponding *squares* were equal
the square of the hypothenuse in the former cases.,

39. This is shown in the above mentioned diagram, No. 34. in which figui
1 shows a triangle having three *acute* angles: that is, the angle a. whic
takes the place of the right angle in the former figures. is *acute*, while i
figure 2. the corresponding angle a is *obtuse*. In each of these figures
is plain to be seen that the two upper (in this case) parallelograms—calle
above diagonal—are together precisely equal to the lower, or right parallel
gram (rectangle), or "oblong square," as Masons call it. Also that th
can be demonstrated by aid of the lines usually drawn, as in other cases c

a right angled triangle or i
the manner last mentione
above. in sections 5 to 8. c
this chapter. or by cutting a
the parallelograms into tr
angles. as shown by th
broken lines. Compare thes
diagrams with those in Nc
21. in this chapter—section
40. These forms may no
only be demonstrated in th
same way. but can be com
bined in all respects the sam

FIG. NO. 1          FIG. NO. 2

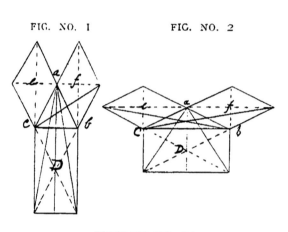

DIAGRAM NO. 34

as the parts of the figure on the Master's carpet. It may be seen from thes
two figures that they may be conjoined with two more like them. and dis
played east, west, north and south to form one rectangle ("oblong square"
of the hypothenuse of each set, precisely the same as the squares of the hy
pothenuse of each set in case of the regular figure of the 47th problem. Com
pare the following diagram, No. 35, with No. 9 and No. 10, in the chapte
concerning "The Form and Situation of the Lodge," and it will be seen tha
the F∴C∴Lodge may be laid out in strict conformity to the regular figure o
the 47th problem; in which the floor is composed of the two squares of the
hypothenuse of the two figures drawn east and west, as shown, and also
conformably in every respect to figures 1 and 2, in diagram 34. with the differ-

ence in this case, No. 35, that the floor is formed by the *one* "oblong square." belonging to all four of the figures drawn in oblong form, east, west, north and south, precisely as in the case of the Master's floor, as shown in diagram No. 19, in Chapter VII, which floor consists of one "perfect square."

41. This variation, as it might be termed, of the 47th problem is one in which the two "sides" of the triangle opposite the longest side are *equal* in length, and in this respect they correspond with the two sides which form the *right angle* in the form inscribed on the Master's carpet. The *squares*

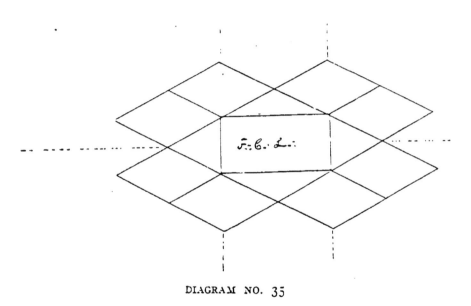

DIAGRAM NO. 35

in the one case and parallelograms in the other, alike take their peculiar angles, and consequently their several forms, from this angle at the intersection of the two equal sides, which angle in each instance might be said to generate the distinguishing features of the two forms throughout.

This is a matter to be borne in mind, as it has to do with the *symbolic* signification involved in the problem as presented in Masonry, which subject will be considered further on. It is also necessarily involved in the explanation of the second and third Great Lights, which, like all other *geometric* symbols, derive their chief significance from the angle or *angles* they display; that is, their intrinsic value as correspondences is *inherent* in the angle.

It is, hence, not for the gratification of mere curiosity that this last explanation is introduced, for it will be seen, on close examination, that it forms a necessary part of the whole subject-matter of the chapter, and to omit it would be to leave this part of the work more incomplete than it would otherwise be, and the intrinsic character of the two Great Lights as *symbols* or representatives, greatly disparaged.

42. But, leaving some further considerations to be disposed of in other chapters, the next and last form of these problems will be still more briefly shown, if possible, before taking up the Masonic uses of the principles involved.

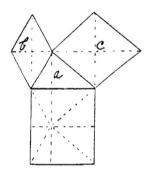

DIAGRAM NO. 36

This last phase of the subject is the triangle having *no right angle, nor any two sides of equal length,* which is, therefore, more different than any from the right angled triangle of equal sides. The next diagram, No. 36, shows the triangle a, with a diamond shaped (rhombus) parallelogram formed on each of the two shorter sides, and marked b and c respectively—each standing diagonally to the oblong or rectangle drawn on the longest (lowest) side (hypothenuse), which last mentioned rectangle stands perpendicular, and the two diagonal parallelograms above, containing together the same area as the lower one, the rectangle or "oblong square"— the same as in the case of the regular figure of the 47th problem. And this can be demonstrated by the broken lines, by noticing that every triangle formed by them in *both* the upper parallelograms is exactly of the same base and altitude as one in the lower; which last is very nearly, but not quite, square, the triangle a being almost a right angled one. In all these figures the principal triangle is just one fourth in area of the principal rectangle (of the hypothenuse), as can be seen by the broken lines in diagram 36.

This last figure has no Masonic or other signification, so far as I know, except to somewhat further illustrate the lesson conveyed by the others, that the right angle *alone* is the angle of *justice,* and by no other can the perfect breastplate of *right*eousness be formed.

43. Of all the geometric figures esteemed in Masonry, there is none which shows the relations between the laws of geometry and those of other sciences more clearly than the figure of the 47th problem. Although this has always been preserved on the Master's carpet, and continually referred to as something of the highest importance to the Craft, I have never known a Mason to study the problem *for* the *purpose of acquiring knowledge in Masonry*. The greater number of Masons of this time can not give any reason why it should be esteemed more than other geometric figures or forms; nor, indeed, why anything of geometry should be preserved in the Lodge, except as a *vague symbol* of some general truth, supposed to be well enough known without it. If asked *where* it appears on the Master's carpet, except where it is expressly placed *conspicuously* as a symbol, they could not answer, and should they seek it they would not find it. They can see on the carpet and in the Monitors three figures, supposed to represent the three Lodges, with certain numbers accompanying them. They do not notice that the figure which stands for the Master's Lodge is nothing but the 47th problem of Euclid a little disguised; nor do they notice that the *false* perspective shown in the *roof* of the Lodge in the figure arises from its being a drawing of said problem with slightly curved lines, and not a representation of the inside of a room, as generally supposed. To show the latter, those lines should not cross as they do at *a* in diagram No. 37.

DIAGRAM NO. 37

44. In this diagram certain perspective lines in what appear to be the floor deceive the eye, as does also the pointed arch above.

This representation shows that the idea of the 47th problem is intimately connected with the *Master's Lodge*. Compare the diagram, No. 37, here shown, with that on the Master's carpet or in the Monitors, and also with diagram 20, in the chapter concerning "the form and situation of the Lodge," and the signification of diagram 37 will be plain. This also shows how extremely careful were the Masters of former times in exposing any information concerning the *Craft* of Masonry to the public, and throws some light on the probable manner in which they kept their *records,* in cases in which they deemed it *proper* to keep *any* whatever.

14

45. Any one, in examining the figures in the Monitors, can notice tha there are two lines in it wholly *out* of *place* as perspective lines of the interic of an arched chamber, viz., those running from the top corners of the interic square and *crossing* to form a *pointed* arch at the rear, and thence running one to the *middle* of each side of the roof at the front or exterior arch. Thes are utterly out of place in the figure taken as a perspective view of an interio but just what they ought to be to show the 47th problem. I often noticed the false figure they show of the form of the arched roof without thinking of this meaning, until I was drawing a figure of the breastplate of Aaron, in conformity to the 47th problem, but with *curved lines,* as the figure requires—when I thought of the meaning of the curved lines in this figure in the Monitors.

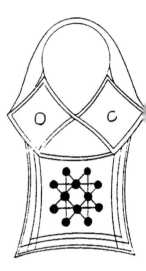

The diagram here given, No. 38, shows the breastplate proper, forming the square of the hypothenuse, and the other two squares, those of the two sides of the right angled triangle, being on the forward part of the shoulders, and containing in their centers the two onyx or beryl stones, believed to be the *"Urim vae Thummim,"* and which

DIAGRAM NO. 38

are termed in the Bible description, "Stones of Memorial." (Exodus, xxviii 12, and xxxix, 7.

46. It is well known that the precious stones (truths) of the breastplate of Aaron were twelve in number, twelve being the product of four *multipliec* by three; and, consequently, as shown in a preceding section (23) of this chapter, the number of *completeness;* as seven, which is the *sum of four* and *three added* together, is the number of *perfection.* It would seem from Exodus, xxviii, 30, that the "Urim vae Thummim" were put into the breastplate when folded up, and therefore some suppose that the twelve stones are meant.

Nothing is said in the books of Moses concerning the order of position of the twelve stones, except that they were set in *four rows,* and that there were *three* in *each row;* that is, doubtless (considering all that appears to have been connected with the breastplate and its jewels)—*two* rows *horizontal* and *two perpendicular,* which arrangement of them would be the most proper order.

The stones had engraved upon them the *names* of the *Israelitish tribes,* *one name* on *each stone.* This breastplate was made *in connection* with the *building* of the *Tabernacle;* and in the *same connection* the *twelve tribes* were *located* in their encampment in a *certain* order, and also had a certain *order* of *march.* Four of the tribes were considered *principal* tribes of the twelve; and with each of the four were associated *two others.* making a group of *three,* in this order: First, JUDAH, with *Issachar* second. *Zebulon* third. Second. REUBEN, with *Simeon* second and *Gad* third. Third, EPHRAIM, with *Manassah* second and *Benjamin* third. Fourth, DAN, with *Asher* second and *Naphtali* third. These four groups were each denominated a "camp," and they were located on the *four sides* of the Tabernacle in this order (see Numbers, chapter ii, verses 2 to 31) : The camp of JUDAH on the *east*—of REUBEN on the *south*—EPHRAIM on the *west*—DAN on the *north.* Their order of *rank* was *Judah* first, *Reuben* second, *Ephraim* third, *Dan* fourth. Their order of *march* was the same, Judah in front, then Reuben, Ephraim, Dan. (See diagram No. 39.)

47. The *"rows"* (as they are called in our Bibles) in which these stones were set seem to be taken for granted to be four straight *horizontal* rows; and our Royal Arch breastplate is composed of twelve oblong slabs of various colored stones, or imitations of stones. In our Monitors and Bible illustrations the stones assigned to the *four principal tribes* are all placed *first,* that is, at the *left* hand in each row, Judah in the top row, Reuben in the next lower, and so on, so that *all four* are on the *same* (north) side of the breastplate. But the *stations* of the standards of the *four camps* are at the *four cardinal points,* the Tabernacle being in the *center.* Hence the four *horizontal* rows, besides leaving no place for the Tabernacle, utterly destroy the *order* in which the tribes were situated when stationary, and also all symbolic meaning belonging to the *jewels,* and particularly their representation of what was signified by this order in the relative positions of the *four camps.* Indeed, the whole invention, besides being altogether contrary to the order

in which the tribes were *purposely* placed, is extremely clumsy and without
any Masonic or other significance, so far as *form* or *position* is concerned,
although both these were deemed of the *highest importance* in every mode
of symbolic representation known to the ancient Hebrews—witness the spe-
cial attention bestowed on *forms* and *positions* in the designs of the Tabernacle and Temple. Whatever "mistakes" Moses may be charged with by
those who may choose to censure him, he surely should not be accused of get-
ting up a Chapter breastplate.

48. In the position given to the twelve stones in the last foregoing diagram, No. 38, they form "*four* rows and *three* in a row," and, besides this,
the stations of the four principal tribes are at the *four cardinal points* about
the *center.* The eight other tribes are at the extreme angles of the Octalpha,
the eight angled *endless triangle* which contains, as above shown, the 47th
problem of Euclid *four fold*—the center (the place of the tabernacle) being
the middle point of the hypothenuse line of each of the right angled triangles.
For these matters see sections 20-25 of this chapter, which sections, and those
concerning diagram No. 38, are parts of one subject.

49. Diagram No. 30 shows the *Octalpha,* or eight angled endless triangle,
with a line drawn from one extreme angle to the next all around (also a
circle circumscribed on the same), by the addition of which straight lines con-
necting the extreme angles a, b, c, etc., the figure is made to contain *twelve*
complete figures of the 47th problem, as explained in section 23. But in the
next hereafter following diagram, No. 39, it is shown that the angles of the
Octalpha, on which the twelve precious stones fall, are each on the *center*
of a *stone* of the *Master's* floor, and in such order that every *alternate* stone
of the floor is occupied by one of the stones of the breastplate, and, there
being twenty-five stones necessarily in the Master Mason's floor, as shown in
the chapters on "the Form and Situation" and on "the Floors of the Lodge,"
this number (25), when divided by taking out every alternate stone, gives
*twelve*, with *thirteen* remaining, that is, *twelve even numbered* and *thirteen
odd* numbered stones; and the thirteen consist of *twelve not* on the center and
the *thirteenth* the *one on* the *center*, which last is the "Stone of *Foundation.*"
This stone, it will be seen, is the only one which is not touched by *any line,*
either of the figure of the Octalpha or of the border.

50. In this diagram, No. 39, the dotted line which runs along the centers of the *outside* row of stones of the floor, all around, is the *inside* line of the border. Within this border line is the floor proper; outside of it the border. The other dotted lines show the Octalpha, the eight angled endless triangle. The eight points of the Octalpha come exactly on this border line, and each of them, and every crossing of the lines, square or diagonal, falls on the center of a *stone* of the floor. On the center of the "Stone of Foundation" (the white stone in the center) is the place of the Tabernacle—on the east, Judah, with Issachar and Zebulon—on the south, Reuben, with Simeon and Gad—on the west, Ephraim, with Manassah and Benjamin, and on the north, Dan, with Asher and Naphtali, each group of three forming a *triad*, and also a *triangle,* toward one of the four *cardinal points.* Each of the four principal tribes is at the *right angle* of its *own camp*, and next the *center;* and the tribe which ranks *second* in the triad is at the *right* and backward from the principal tribe, and the third tribe of the camp rearward on the left, as we look from their "camp" *toward* the center—that is, that the triads en-

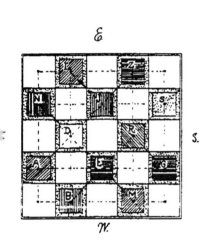

DIAGRAM NO. 39

camped each facing *towards* the *Tabernacle,* which was at the center. In the central space around the court of the Tabernacle the *Levites* encamped. They were divided into *three* divisions, the descendants of the three sons of Levi, viz., Gershon, Kohath and Merari.

These three divisions of the tribe of Levi had each separate duties to perform in caring for and carrying the parts and furniture of the tabernacle and the court. When the march began, the camp of Judah set forward, and the sons of *Gershon* and *Merari* next, with the tabernacle; next followed the camp of Reuben; then the sons of *Kohath,* with the "sanctuary" (the sanctified furniture and symbols, etc.)—next the camp of Ephraim, and lastly the camp of Dan. (See Numbers, x, 14 to 28, and Numbers, ii, 2 to 31.)

51. In diagram 39 the colors of the four principal tribes, Judah, Reuber Ephraim and Dan, are given, according to the Royal Arch legend, red, purple blue and white. The confusion in the names and colors of the preciou stones, as given by various authors, is such, as to most of them, that any on may take his choice as to which color he will assign to any tribe. Those her given are each according to some authority and contrary to others, but they will answer the purpose of variety, which is the best that one can be certain of. The colors of the stones are represented in diagram 39, as in heraldry, by the fine lines and dots of the surface, viz.—white is blank—blue, close hori zontal lines—red, perpendicular lines—purple, diagonal from upper left t lower right corner—green, diagonal lines from upper right to lower left—gray, horizontal lines more open than blue—yellow, white, dotted with black.

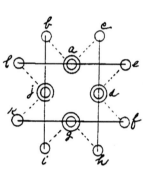

DIAGRAM NO. 40

52. It is manifest that if the tribes are to be represented in the breastplate in the order of their encampment, the four principal tribes *must* be placed as shown in diagram No. 39, for one was located at the *east*, one at the *south*, one at the *west* and one at the *north*, so they could *not* have encamped in four *parallel* and *even rows*. But each principal tribe was princi- pal of a division, having two others joined or brigaded with it; and they *three* formed one "*camp*." And they must all have been arranged so as not to *inter- lock* with or encroach upon the ground of each other. Hence, in order that there might be *four rows* or *four groups* of any order, the three tribes of each camp must have formed a triangle *on its own side* of the *center*, as in diagram 39; and by this very form they would fall into four *rows*, with three in a row, as well as form *triangles*, as may be seen in said figure, where there are *two rows* horizontal and two perpendicular, and these are the only *rows* which can be on *four* sides of a center. But these rows *cross* each other; and while that is all right, as far as having the stones in perfect symbolic order is concerned, yet the *three* tribes forming *each camp* must be so placed that the several camps can fall together *without crossing each other's ground*, and conse- quently each *row* is not *one camp*, but each *triangle* is, as shown in diagram 40.

at a, b, c,—d. e, f.—g, h, i.—j, k, l, while the *rows* are a, e, l,—d, c, h,— g, f, k,—j, i, b.  Thus each of the four principal *standards* of the camps comes in the *middle* position, on the cardinal point, facing the tabernacle, *both* in the *row* and in the *triangle;* and each *tribal standard* of all the other *eight* is aligned *four* ways—in two ways as one of *two,* in one way as one of *three,* and in one way as one of *four*—and *besides* is *one* of *its own triad,* which form its *triangle,* and the standards of the *four principals* are in a greater number of combinations.  Besides, are the relations of all to the *twelve* figures of the 47th problem, which appear when the lines of the Octalpha are completed as in diagram 39, and especially diagram 30.

53.  It is well known that if many Master Masons, to say nothing of Masters of Lodges, were asked, What has the 47th problem of Euclid to do with the floor of the Master's Lodge? they could give no particular answer, because they do not know that the floor of either Lodge is in any conformity to the globe of the earth, and the astronomic lines which mark the apparent course of the sun upon the earth; nor how the lines of the Lodge conform to the square of the hypothenuse of a right angled triangle projected on a certain scale; nor how the stones of the floors of all the Lodges are to be placed, in order to give the "stone of foundation" its proper place; nor how all lines of every Lodge, and all angles as well of the problem of Euclid as of the Lodge floors, and the astronomic lines and poles of the earth, fall upon the *centers* of their proper stones; nor how the border of every Lodge floor is formed; nor why it is called a "border of scroll work;" nor what connection the scroll work has with the figure of the 47th problem; nor how the Royal arch is formed from the figure of the problem, with its proper circles; nor how the Master's floor conforms to the nine circles (arches) of Enoch, with the stone of foundation contained in the ninth arch; nor what the 47th problem has to do with the positions of the Great Lights; nor what difference is consequently to be observed in placing the same in each Degree; nor what squares are to be used in the first and second; nor why they must be *oblong;* nor what difference in their positions in each Degree; and, more important than all, what, and how executed, is a regular "advance;" nor why "oblong" and "perfect squares" are necessary in the same; nor how the square of the hypothenuse falls in each case; nor where, nor what, is the

position of the center; nor how the square of the Master Mason's hypothenuse contains the "stone of foundation;" nor why it is that the square of the hypothenuse of the E∴A∴ and F∴C∴ *never can* contain the *center,* and consequently the stone of foundation; nor that when our elders spoke of "the Master's square" and "the Fellow Craft's square," they spoke of the *hypothenuse* thereof; nor how the equilateral triangle, as well as the right angled triangle, conforms to the nine circles (arches) of Enoch; nor that our ancient brethren were speaking of geometry when they put forth the legend (so called) of "the nine arches of Enoch" and the "stone of foundation," and said that the latter was "first *revealed* in *heaven,*" and that Enoch put the *"secrets* of *geometry"* in *"two great pillars,"* etc.

54. And the same is the case in respect to the matters not specially connected with the 47th problem; as these, that they do not know that circumambulation is around and *outside* of the Lodge, and *not inside* of it; that if the W∴M∴ and Wardens are inside the gates of the Lodge, anything done between their stations, that is, within the *four cardinal points,* is done *in the Lodge;* nor that this innovation has been made within the last fifty or sixty years in this country *only;* nor why the *north* (in the *first* Degree) is called the place of *darkness,* when that is the place of *prudence;* nor that prudence and darkness each means *hiding;* nor what any one of the *salutations* signifies; nor that the *whole* of the *omnific* word is *concealed* in the Lodge *to this day,* together with its *"heling"* words; nor what are the significations of the signs.

55. From what is implied above, if such implication be well founded, there seems to be abundant reason why the art of Masonry should be based on the science of geometry, and why that should be the science of sciences in such a system. And from the foregoing chapters, and what follows herein, why the problem of the right angled triangle should hold the highest place in the esteem of all well-informed Masons, and also why so much is claimed for the expression that "Masonry is *founded* in *geometry.*"

In order to ascertain, to some limited extent, whether or not there are any characteristic principles in geometry, by which may be discovered the correspondences between material things and the laws of their processes and operations on the one hand, and things of the intellectual and voluntary

PLATE XII.

The Maltese Cross, Showing the Master's Floor and Border and Outer
Line of the Lowest Floor and Eight of the Smaller Sixteen Triangles,
Two on Each Side of the Floor, Forming One Beam or One Arm of
the Cross.  The Stone of Foundation and the Ninth Circle of Enoch.

powers of man and the laws of their processes and operations on the other, let us glance first at a few instances showing the correspondence between the laws of geometry and those of some of the physical and natural sciences, so far as they may be simply and readily illustrated by the principles of the 47th problem.

56. Take the figure of the same, first mentioned in this chapter—a right angle of *equal* sides—(see figure 1 of diagram No. 21, section 3 of this chapter), and the operation of two *equal* forces, meeting at a right angle, as the two sides of the squares, 1 and 2, meet at a. Then by the dynamical laws which regulate the composition and resolution of forces we find that the compound or resulting force, that is, the force remaining of the two original forces, not counteracted and annulled by their collision, will take the direction of the perpendicular broken line a, f (which is a continuation of the dotted line g, a), the direction of the line of movement of each original

FIG. 1 FIG. 2 FIG. 1 FIG. 2

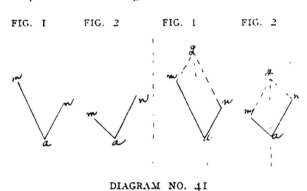

DIAGRAM NO. 41

force being diverted 45 degrees. The square a. m. g. n. will be what is termed the "parallelogram of forces," which is thus formed. Let the two lines m a and n a, in either of the two figures 1 and 2 on the left, in the next following diagram, No. 41, represent two distinct forces, which meet at a; the *direction* of each line shows the *direction* of the force, and the *length* shows the *intensity* of the same. Thus, in figure 1 on the left, the force m a is about twice as great as the force n a, while in figures 2, same side, the force n a is about twice as great as m a. By repeating these two figures on the right, and drawing the broken lines g m and g n in each case, a parallelogram is formed, which is the "parallelogram of forces" mentioned above. The use of this is to show the *direction* and intensity of the force which *results* from the union of the two original forces, which is done by drawing the broken line g a diagonally through each parallelogram. The *direction* of this last line shows the *direction* of the resultant force, and the *length* of the same from g to a, which is called the "*diagonal* of forces," shows the *intensity* or *sum* of that force, as compared with the lines m a and n a in each case.

57. Now, to return to the figure of the 47th problem, in diagram 21. Take figure 1 of that diagram, and let the two whole lines of equal length. m a and n a, represent two *equal* forces meeting at right angles at a; then the two dotted lines m g and n g, being added, form the parallelogram of forces, which in this case is a perfect *square,* and the same in size as either of the upper diagonal squares 1 and 2 on the two sides of the triangle; and the dotted line g a will be the diagonal of forces, and its direction, which is *perpendicular.* will show the *direction* of the resulting force, and its length. which is the *same* as the *hypothenuse* of the triangle, will show the *sum* or intensity of the force, as in the other cases in diagram No. 41. Consequently. the length of either *side* of the parallelogram of forces, which is the same as the length of either side of either diagonal squares 1 or 2, will be to the length of the hypothenuse as the *intensity* of either of the original forces is to the intensity of the composed or resultant force. This proportion is always, in a case of *this kind.* the same as the diameter of a circle inscribed in any given square is to the diameter of a circle circumscribed on the same square. which is the same as the proportion existing between the sides of each of the squares 1 and 2 and the sides of the square (3) of the hypothenuse, and the same as the diameter or circumference of any one of the nine circles heretofore mentioned is to that of the next larger circle.

58. However, these proportions are *directly* as the *length* and not as the *squares* of the lines, as in the case of the *areas* of the three *squares* or oblongs and square of the 47th problem. But this is well enough, for in using the proportions of the *squares* we seek to ascertain *areas,* which is not the case as to forces, except we experiment with them as to their distribution over given spaces, when their operation is by means of elastic vapors, as steam, and their diffusion in respect to distance, and proportionate diminution in consequence, and the like. Further, if *squares* should be drawn on the two principal *side lines* and the diagonal of the parallelogram of forces, they would show the same proportion in area as the squares in the figures of the 47th problem; for these last are drawn on the two sides of the triangle,

nd on the hypothenuse, which *is* the *diagonal,* when the two sides lacking
re added to make the triangle a "perfect square." All this is shown by
figures 1 and 2 in the same diagram, No. 21, and by the next here following
diagram, No. 42, which is similar to No. 2, with one additional rectangle, ii,
being composed of the triangle i and its counterpart ii, formed by dotted
lines. Here 1, 2 and 3 are the square of the 47th problem; *a m g n* is the
parallelogram of forces; *c cc* are two right angled triangles, each exactly
qual to i, the triangle of the figure of the problem, and to *ii,* the dotted
triangle below it; *g a* is the diagonal of the parallelogram of forces, which
represents the *direction* and *sum* of the resultant force, produced by the forces
*n a* and *n a;* 1 and 2 are the squares of the sides of the right angled triangle i of the problem, and are also the squares of the
lines m a and n a, which represent the two original acting
forces, their *intensity* and *direction.* The diagonal **g a**
represents the *intensity* or *sum* of the combined or composed forces, and also the *direction* of the same. The
length of this diagonal is the same as that of b c, the
*hypothenuse*—hence the square of **g a** is equal to the
square 3, which is the square of the hypothenuse.

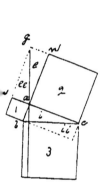

DIAGRAM NO. 42

While the foregoing observations concerning forces
are intended to illustrate the scope of the 47th problem,
that is, a figure formed on a *right* angled triangle, either
f equal or unequal sides, it is clear that the principles involved are ap-
licable to the other forms shown in diagrams 34, 35, 36, in which the triangle
xhibited has no right angle, as is sufficiently plain from the parallelograms
n diagram No. 41, in which the angles are acute and obtuse—all which goes
o show the direct and intimate connection between the laws of geometry and
nose of physical force.

59. That the directions in which natural forces move under all conditions
f complication are in accordance with the laws of geometry is well known,
nd the solution of the countless problems growing out of such conditions
ffords abundant examples of the co-ordination of the laws of that science
rith those of the science of numbers.

The paths of the planets and other heavenly bodies, variable as they are under the combined and shifting attractions of each other, are all compelled by resultant forces to continually assume and maintain some form of the section of a cone. That is, when any cone is cut asunder the figure which bounds the cut surface is termed a *section* of that particular cone, for cones are of various lengths, in proportion to the diameter of their bases, and the section or cutting may be in *any direction* through any part of the cone. Hence, by cutting, innumerable forms, including the triangle, parabola, hyperbola, ellipse and circle, may be obtained, and all of these of various dimensions, and all, except the circle and triangle, of various forms—the triangle by cutting perpendicularly from the *apex* to the *base,* and the circle by cutting *horizontally, parallel* to the base, which is the circle itself; and the other forms by cutting in various directions obliquely to the base. All these are here mentioned to further illustrate what was said above in several places, that the triangle is the *simplest* form possible, of which all other forms are composed, and having the *least* area in proportion to the linear extent of its boundary or periphery; while the circle is the most *comprehensive* form possible, in which all other forms are contained, as it has the *greatest* area in proportion to the extent of its boundary or circumference. These two stand at *right angles* to each other in the cone. One must reach the *apex,* and the other may be at right angles to it anywhere between the apex and the base. The *triangle* and *circle* are the two extreme figures, as we might say, of the geometrical *gamut,* or scale, which correspond by their forms severally to the respective *sounds,* that is, the *fullest* and *sharpest* natural *notes* of the musical octave, which has its three principal notes. Also, to the extremes of the octave of colors, which has its three principal ones, which are *red, blue* and *yellow,* and doubtless, also, to the scales of tastes and odors.

The *three* corresponding grades of form in geometry, and consequently in Masonry, are the *circle,* the *square* and the *triangle.*

The parts of any cone, when cut, may be laid with the cut surface flat on a sheet of paper, and the boundary of the section traced, and thus it will appear that bodies moving on any of the curves so drawn must of necessity move according to the laws of geometry, by which such surface can be measured; and if the bodies so move under the impulse of various forces in complication, it is clear that the forces themselves proceed in accordance with corresponding laws of geometry, otherwise confusion, and often collision, must result.

60. And these laws pursue all matter, into whatsoever position or combination any portion of it may be found—whether in great masses, as those composing the globes of heaven, or in small, minute, or even infinitesimal particles, down to atoms; whether in separate, mingled or combined forms, and whether the conformity they actually observe to such laws be apparent at first sight, or only discoverable by patient investigation.

Accordingly there arises an endless multitude of cases in forming compounds and mixtures, which, though they may not appear to have any relation to the laws of geometry, are in fact governed throughout in all which relates to form, attraction, repulsion, expansion, condensation, position, proper and local motion, and many other matters, by those very laws, and in many respects and countless instances by the principles involved in the problem here under consideration.

61. In not a few cases we can discern results which flow by very secret processes from the operation of these principles. Take, for example, the mingling of colors. If red and blue be mingled in *equal* quantities the product will be an equal mixture, and the color of it will be purple. And whatever the quantity of the blue compared with the red, the mixture will be more blue or more red in proportion; and what may be called the *sum* of the purple will in all cases be equal to that of both ingredients, unless there be some cause which neutralizes a portion of one or both the latter upon their mixture, comparatively as in the case of forces upon their collision at various angles.

These results are *direct*, and not according to the *squares*. Yet, if we take the surface which the pigments will color to a given degree of intensity, they will compare according to area covered with color, as the areas of the squares in the 47th problem compare. But these matters are mentioned because they are so familiar that no one thinks of their having any connection with geometry.

62. Chemical combinations, also, which are very different from mixtures, are doubtless formed according to the laws of geometry, no matter what may be the cause of those unaccountable attractions and repulsions which the dif-

ferent elementary substances. as well as their compounds, exhibit towards each other.

If the ultimate atoms of divers kinds of matter form themselves into particles, and these into corpuscles or molecules, and these again into bodies less and less minute, up to those which may be visible to the naked eye. they must take place in every such collocation in *positions* relative to the *place* of each other, and so present themselves in geometric forms, let the composition be what or of what degree it may. This is the case with crystals of every kind; they assume various forms, but each substance or compound presents forms peculiar to itself, and always the same, so that one crystal will be a cube, and that of another substance a tetrahedron, and so on, and all these forms are geometric.

63. Their combinations, primary and secondary, etc., are conformed to those inexplicable laws which pervade all the realm of matter, even to its ultimates, and the principles which rule are in correspondence with those of the 47th problem. Of this there can be no doubt, as order, to exist at all in complications and co-operations so infinitely vast. multifarious and minute as necessarily exist throughout the domain of matter, must admit of nothing less than the most exquisite *precision* and *conformity* in all respects and relations, through and through; otherwise chaos would be instantly and constantly present in the very heart of every conceivable thing of the material universe.

64. The same laws which govern forces, chemical operations, crystallization, winds, waves and explosions, must govern musical sounds, and the vibrations of solids, liquids and fluids, which produce them, and indeed all sounds produced in any manner, whether musical or not.

The correspondence between the conjunction and collision of waves of sound, and of forces of whatsoever kind, can be detected to a satisfactory extent by all who are familiar with the motions, reflections and counteractions known to take place in liquids and fluids, all which movements are **caused by** the direct and reflex and combined action of forces, and the laws **of motion are** always uniform in the same subject. The movements they **cause in** any physical mass or medium whatever must also conform to their own laws. Hence, there can be no doubt that all the motions possible in the universe may be mapped out in geometric forms and order.

65. So much being suggested as to the kinship which exists between the laws of things treated of in the different sciences—natural, physical and abstract—it remains to consider briefly what, if any, correspondence exists between the principles of physical and natural laws and those of metaphysical truths and facts—between the order of corporeal, material things and agencies, and the incorporeal, spiritual powers and agencies, and their respective forms, modes and operations.

66. Such correspondence is mentioned in chapter No. V, concerning "Geometry," sections 12 to 22, and some suggestions made as to the order of the universe being similar to itself in all its parts; and also in chapter VI, concerning the "Three Great Lights." But as the 47th problem of Euclid is chosen in Masonry as the most complete of all simple examples in geometry which can be used for the illustration of these truths, something further will be proper in this chapter to follow the illustrations hereinabove contained—something which will show more fully and clearly how it is that *man himself* is in the constitution and co-ordination of the powers, faculties and operations of his moral (voluntary) and intellectual complex, what might be termed a counterpart or similitude, by correspondence, of the geometric forms and principles involved in the problem figured on the Master's carpet. and the relations which they sustain to each other.

67. The right angled triangle in the geometric figure mentioned is that form from which, or by which, the three squares drawn upon its sides may be said to be generated. Two of the squares touch each other at the right angle of the triangle, where the lines which form the right angle meet, and each of these being extended or produced beyond that point, they *cross* at right angles, and *each* thus becomes *one* line of *each* of the *two* squares. The third and longest line (hypothenuse) *unites* the two other points of the triangle, and consequently two other angles of the same two squares which lie on its two sides, and on this third side or line is drawn the *third* square, one of its *corners* touching a corner of *each* of the other squares, the *triangle* forming *one line* of *each* of the *three;* and the combined area of the first and second, that is, what they contain, no matter what may be the difference

between them, is always equal to the area of the third. The three are alway in *contact* by the lines which bound them, and the first two, as it were, flov into and fill the third. How much soever their relative sizes may be changed they will still furnish just enough surface to equal that of the third square, s long as the right angle is maintained.

68. As is the *direction* of the lines of the *right* angle relatively to an, given line—say, the *equator,* which runs due *east* and west—so is the *righ* or *oblique* position of the several squares as to such line. If the lines of th right angle are of *equal* length, and *oblique* to the *equator* at an angle of 4; degrees, the *square* of the *hypothenuse* will be *right* (square) with the *equa tor* and *meridian,* those two unchangeable lines of the Lodge *floor,* by whicl every thing thereon is "*oriented.*" Consequently this square will be such that those two lines may *cross* upon its *center, squarely* with its own lines. But if the side lines of the *triangle* be of *unequal* length, the squares formed or them will be of *unequal area,* and the *right angle* retaining its position or *obliquity* of 45 degrees, the *square* of the *hypothenuse* can not be square with the *equator* or *meridian,* and consequently they can not cross on its *center, square* with its own lines; and if the two sides in such case be *square* with the equator and meridian, still the square of the hypothenuse will not be square with them, but *oblique.* In Masonic language, the right angle will be that of an "oblong square," and the square of its hypothenuse can never be "on the center." Here it may begin to appear what is intended by the last above two sections. See section 32 of chapter V, entitled "Geometry," and diagram No. 4. Bear in mind that *all "oblong* squares" in Masonry, when horizontal, are square with the *equator* and *meridian.*

Hence it is necessary that the Lodge should be laid out conformably to the *fixed lines of the earth;* otherwise the processes of its Degrees would be like a survey regulated by a compass, if there were *no magnetic pole* to which it should conform, and consequently confusion, so abhorrent to Masonry, would be the result.

69. It must be further borne in mind that in Masonry every geometric position or form which relates to the Lodge is *oriented;* that is, placed and formed to correspond with the lines of the Lodge, that is, of the earth, viz., the astronomic lines shown in the chapter on the form and situation of the

Lodge and elsewhere; and if this were not done, the Degrees would be *unfastened* as well as unfixed, and utterly dissipated in their very inception.

Consequently the right angled triangle, as the Degree and work may require, is disposed in the cases here to be understood in conformity to the proper lines. If it were not so, no proper order could be maintained, and the right angle being allowed to *shift* its *position* (as has come to pass in our Lodges), *any* square of any hypothenuse might (and now often does) fall conformably to the equator and meridian, and *vice versa*. This is what is meant above when it is said that the two *sides* of the right angled triangle must be of *equal length*, in order that the square of the hypothenuse may fall conformably to the proper lines, on the center—that is, provided every square of *the three* be properly oriented according to its Degree. This is as much as can be said on this subject in this place. What is lacking must be supplied by that "skill and assiduity" which in this case "will *not go unrewarded*." But in the two oblong floors the squares (oblong) which are formed must be square with the meridian and tropical lines—the hypothenuse *otherwise*.

70. Let us now consider man in relation to the Degrees and principles involved *in him* as a *metaphysical problem*, as we have above considered the forms and principles involved in the 47th Euclid as a geometric problem, and note the correspondence between them. To do this let us begin, as in the former case, with the *triangle*.

Recollect that the *equilateral* triangle, as shown in the chapter covering the "Three Great Lights," is in Masonry the representative of *essence* itself—that which has *life in itself*—the self-existing and *only* life—consequently the Divine Being. Further, that the *right angled* triangle is the representative of the *existence, works, operations*, of the Divine *Being* or esse. Hence the life, viz., *existence*, of man, or any finited being higher or lower than he, is represented by the *right angled* triangle, either of equal sides, as that belonging to the M∴Mason's Degree, or of *unequal* sides or limbs, as that belonging to either of the first two Degrees, which is the same in each, though used necessarily in *reversed* order, as shown above in several places.

71. As the triangle in the problem here discussed is the prime, or first, principle of all, from or by which the several squares are generated, and by its fundamental and *characteristic* property the Degrees in its *right angle*

and the *equality* or *inequality* of its two sides produce or fix the *area* and *position* of the two squares of the same, so the *prime* or first principle in man, derived by *subsistence* from the self-existing, puts itself forth in the two (dual) forms or Degrees thereof, which we know as the *will* and the *understanding*—the *voluntary* and *rational* principles—the moral and intellectual—which two are represented by the two *sides* of man, and which constitute him a man. *These two* are the two *squares* of the sides of the right angle of his problem. corresponding to the two squares of the geometric problem.

72. These two, the will and the understanding, put themselves forth in *operation*. the will being that *from* which and the understanding that *by* which all proceeds, the former being primary and the latter secondary; and their manifestations. in effect, that is, in *volition* and *thought*. acting as *one*. proceed in this very order, so that in their *conjoint operation* they constitute the *third* or *square* of the hypothenuse—the *character*, the *quality* and *sum*, *totality*, *value* of his very life.

As is the *proportion* of the two (primary and secondary) squares to *each other*, such is the *equal* or *unequal* result in the (tertiary) square of the hypothenuse, as shown in No. 21, by division of that square by the line from the right angle perpendicular (at right angles) to the line of the hypothenuse. which always so divides that square that the part of it which lies next to (joins corners with) *either* of the other two squares is exactly *equal* to the same in *area*. that is, contains the same surface. This is why it was mentioned in section 67 that this third square is connected with each of the others at its proper corner. And this connection, in the case of a right angle of equal sides, is also in the order of the composition of forces, for the two lines of either of the two diagonal squares meet to form one *side line* of the square of the hypothenuse, which side line thus is necessarily a *diagonal* to the particular square whose lines so meet to form it. precisely as the diagonal of forces is to the lines representing the original forces in figure 1, diagram No. 21. On the other hand, in No. 2, in same diagram, the upper squares, those of the sides of the triangle. are so *inclined* both to the *same* side. that the diagonals of forces, h c and l b. instead of being *perpendicular* to the hypothenuse, as in figure 1, are thrown obliquely, and yet can not project even an oblique *square*, for they are of different *lengths* by reason of the inequality of the two squares which produce them.

73. Thus the contents of *each* of the *dual* squares of the sides is in geometry represented as to *space* in the square of the hypothenuse by its corresponding rectangle, formed by the above mentioned perpendicular division line. And in like manner in man, in the will and understanding—the moral and intellectual powers—which act together as *dual*, but separately as *double*, are each distinctly recognizable in the operations as well as in the outcome of his life and in all his character.

If the will be weak, vacillating or depraved, such character thereof will be discernible in the results of his intentions and *acts*, even though his intellect be superior. In like manner, though his will be good and strong, if his intellectual powers be naturally deficient, or blunted by superstition or ignorance, the outcome of all he may attempt from first to last will be of little account, and often contemptible.

74. In the one case the square of the hypothenuse formed by or in him falls more or less obliquely to *one* side, and in the other case to the *opposite* side of the *equatorial* line of directness—of truth and *right*—which line is the equivalent representative, in a *horizontal* plane, to the plumb line in a *perpendicular* plane. No one in whom the two essential and inseparable powers and capacities of his life are *unequally* conjoined can face the rising sun, and form or exhibit a square of the hypothenuse, which can quadrate with the unchanging lines, whose four right angles are at the *center*.

Moreover, he can not walk so or where he may ever reach the center. His path is on one side or the other, according to the *Degree* which is dominant in him; nor can he see the East, except *obliquely;* his course is mid "darkness and light," or "lights and darkness," and he arrives at nothing better. The place of lights and perfections is not for him, for it is on the *center*.

75. He only who is on the "perfect square," the right angle of equal limbs, can walk the ordered line, or arrive where the *dual* principles of Good and Truth, derivative and subsistent from the primal and omnific love and wisdom, form to themselves the very *sanctum sanctorum*, whose *length* and *breadth* are *equal*, whose floor is the square of the celestial hypothenuse—"the

Place of Lights and Perfections." All others must pursue their course on th "*lesser circles,*" the *side lines* of inequality (for all circles of the globe, eas and west, save *one,* are "*lesser* circles"), and must halt in *arrested* progres where their lines of imperfect projection fall unconformably with those of th celestial trestle board.

76. He only who has an *equal* mind can be in *equilibrium;* he only ad vances with equipoise of passions and judgment on that way of life whicl is lighted by the unflickering lamp of *truth*—for him, because *in* him the tw great pillars stand in *strength* and *establishment* on the *left* and *right*—to hin the olive wood doors are ever open, and with the waning light of time th inner veils grow more and more translucent to the light of the Shekinah.

Depend upon it, Craftsmen, he goes upon "a chase of the rainbow" whe seeks to find *beyond* the *sanctum sanctorum* of the Master's Lodge something "*higher*" or more sublime in Masonry. It is there, on the *center,* where the Masonic ambulation closes; there Masonic art, science, philosophy and mys tery attain their culmination and *end.* All beyond the three incomparabl Degrees of the ancient Lodge, as they were known to the "worthy and wel qualified" who passed before, and as they should and shall yet be restorec to us or our successors, may be described in those words of ancient utterance "Vanity of vanities, and vexation of spirit"—"for there is nothing *new* un der the *sun.*"

CPSIA information can be obtained at www.ICGtesting.com
Printed in the USA
BVOW060423110713

325614BV00007B/150/P